to Civilization

FINANCIAL MELTDOWNS

Erin L. McCoy

Cavendish Square
New York

Published in 2019 by Cavendish Square Publishing, LLC
243 5th Avenue, Suite 136, New York, NY 10016

Cataloging-in-Publication Data

Names: McCoy, Erin L.
Title: Financial meltdowns / Erin L. McCoy.
Description: New York : Cavendish Square, 2019. |
Series: The top six threats to civilization | Includes glossary and index.
Identifiers: ISBN 9781502640628 (pbk.) | ISBN 9781502640635 (library bound) |
ISBN 9781502640642 (ebook)
Subjects: LCSH: Financial crises–Juvenile literature. |
International finance–Juvenile literature.
Classification: LCC HB3722.M33 2019 | DDC 338.5'42–dc23

Editorial Director: David McNamara
Copy Editor: Alex Tessman
Associate Art Director: Alan Sliwinski
Designer: Ginny Kemmerer
Production Coordinator: Karol Szymczuk
Photo Research: J8 Media

Portions of this book originally appeared in *World Financial Meltdown* by Laura La Bella.

The photographs in this book are used by permission and through the courtesy of: Cover Saul Gravy/ Ikon Images/Getty Images; background used throughout Tflex/Shutterstock.com; background used throughout iulias/Shutterstock.com; 4-5 Trong Nguyen/Shutterstock.com; p. 6 Everett Historical/ Shutterstock.com; p. 8 Mario Tama/Getty Images; p. 11 catnap72/E+/Getty Images; p. 13 Leremy/ Shutterstock.com; p. 14 Photo12/UIG via Getty Images; p. 16 MARIA BASTONE/AFP/Getty Images; p. 18 Chris Hondros/Newsmakers/Getty Images; p. 19 Justin Sullivan/Getty Images; p. 21 Chris Hondros/Getty Images; p. 22 GiovanniMartin16/Wikimedia Commons/File:Historical GDP growth of the United States.png; p. 24 Wit Olszewski Shutterstock.com; p. 26 Andrew Harrer/Bloomberg via Getty Images; p. 30 Spencer Platt/Getty Images; p. 33 Dorothea Lange/Wikimedia Commons/File:LangeMigrantMother02.jpg; p. 36 Kaliva/Shutterstock.com; p. 38 MARK RALSTON/AFP/Getty Images; p. 40 seksan Mongkhonkhamsao/ Moment/Getty Images; p. 41 Spencer Platt/Getty Images; p. 42-43 AP Photo/Mark Humphrey; p. 44 photka/Shutterstock.com; p. 45 igor kisselev/Shutterstock.com; p. 46-47 Nancy Pelosi/Wikimedia Commons/File:President Obama Signs the DoddFrank Wall Street Reform and Consumer Protection Act (4816864266).jpg; p. 48 deepadesigns/Shutterstock.com.

Printed in the United States of America

CONTENTS

INTRODUCTION: THE ECONOMY COLLAPSES

It's time for you to do your weekly grocery shopping, so you stop by your bank on the way to withdraw money. The doors are locked. A sign hangs in the window: "No new withdrawals." You try to take out money from the ATM (automated teller machine) outside the bank and you see the same message. What's going on?

You take out your phone and check the news. It turns out there has been a run on the bank today. The stock market is on the verge of a crash, and it seems people got so worried that they were more comfortable keeping cash under the mattress than leaving it in the bank. This morning, so many people were trying to withdraw money that your bank closed all its branches throughout the country. No one can access their funds.

A WIDESPREAD CRISIS

You still have a credit card, so you go to the grocery store. As you walk down the aisle, many of the items you're looking for are out of stock. You ask the cashier why, and she says that the store can't buy any new

Opposite: Shelves in a Walmart in Humble, Texas, have been cleared out as locals stockpile in preparation for Hurricane Harvey in 2017.

products until it can access its own accounts. You try to pay with your credit card, but it is denied—and now you have no way of making a purchase at all. You head home, hoping there's enough food in the pantry to last you a few days—or longer, if necessary.

At home, you turn on the television. The news reports are shocking. The US banking system is on the brink of collapse. The world economy is crumbling. Debit cards are useless, credit cards no longer work, and getting your money out of the bank—well, good luck. You turn on your computer and attempt to access your bank's website. You are shocked to see that all of your hard-earned money is gone.

A group of depositors protest outside the Bank of United States in New York City in 1931 after the bank's failure at the height of the Great Depression.

The US government can no longer afford to pay the salaries of its employees and military personnel. It shuts down and the country is left vulnerable to attack. Retired seniors who rely on monthly checks from Social Security and Medicare have no income at all now. The news networks show major social upheaval taking place in cities around the world. People are stealing food and supplies, and they're breaking into homes to look for money. Mass hysteria has set in.

THE GREAT RECESSION

How likely is it that a financial meltdown like the worst-case scenario described here could actually occur? Some say that it nearly happened a decade ago.

On September 17, 2008, there was a bank run that brought the US economy close to collapse. Money market accounts are among the safest investments a person can make, but investors were worried. The housing market was crumbling. People were unable to keep up with their payments and the value of homes was dropping. On September 17, following news that investment bank Lehman Brothers was filing for bankruptcy, investors withdrew $144.5 billion from these supposedly safe accounts—a record amount for a single day. Compare that to a normal week, when just around $7 billion is generally withdrawn. Investors wanted to make sure they didn't lose their money.

Businesses keep the money that they use for daily expenses in money market accounts. Luckily, not all the money was withdrawn. "If those funds had run dry, your grocery store shelves would have gone empty within weeks," explains Kimberly Amadeo, an economic analyst and business strategist writing for the *Balance*, an online financial publication. Experts were worried that corporate investors would be the next group

A September 16, 2008, newspaper reports on the worst single day in stock market losses since the September 11, 2001, terrorist attacks.

to withdraw huge sums of money. Treasury Secretary Henry Paulsen and Federal Reserve Chairman Ben Bernanke recommended that Congress pass a bill to spend $700 billion to bail out the banks. Some argued that the banks had made bad decisions and should face the consequences. Others insisted that the American and global economies—not just the banks—would suffer should several large financial institutions fail. The US Congress asked Paulson what would happen next if there was no bailout. "Heaven help us all," he said.

What ensued was the longest economic recession since World War II. During the Great Recession, which lasted from December 2007 through 2009, the average family income dropped 17 percent. The unemployment rate—the number of people without jobs who were willing and able to work—increased from 4.7 percent in the autumn of 2007 to 10 percent in October 2009. Home values plummeted 30 percent between mid-2006 and mid-2009, and many people lost their houses; some individuals and families were left with no other option than to live on the streets.

The bailout bill, passed on October 3, 2008, sought to prevent banks from collapsing under a great deal of debt incurred as a result of granting or taking on loans that could not be repaid. It also kept large companies such as General Motors and Chrysler from going bankrupt. In the end, President Barack Obama chose not to use about half the $700 billion bailout money. In any case, all the companies that were lent money were required to pay it back, though many still had not done so as of April 2018, according to a balance sheet kept by *ProPublica*, a nonprofit investigative journalism website. Meanwhile, the American Recovery and Reinvestment Act, passed in February 2009, invested $787 billion in an economic stimulus plan aimed at increasing consumer spending, cutting taxes, and saving jobs. Nearly a decade later, the economy has recovered, and while opinions vary on whether the stimulus package and the bailout helped this to happen, most agree that the crisis could have been a lot worse.

Whether another financial meltdown, even worse than the last, is in our future is a matter for debate. Some say that key legislation is required to prevent banks from making the same kinds of risky loans, and to keep them from doing what caused the recession: repackaging these mortgages to look less risky than they were, then reselling them. Others insist that such laws hurt business growth.

Many argue that a full-scale financial meltdown is unlikely. They say that a free-market economy—that is, an economic system in which businesses compete openly, without restriction—would help keep businesses in check. The next financial meltdown—when and if it comes—may be hard to foresee, but possible to prevent.

CHAPTER 1
A BRIEF HISTORY OF ECONOMIC CRISES

The Great Recession was not the first financial meltdown that the world has experienced, nor is it likely to be the last. However, the scale of such collapses can vary dramatically. Most agree that, while the Great Recession was a disaster for many, a much more devastating economic disaster was narrowly averted. Are such doomsday disaster scenarios worth worrying about, or are they just designed to scare us? How can we determine just how likely they are? A look back at the history of similar events can help us understand the causes of such catastrophic occurrences and offer insight into how to prevent them.

DEFINING ECONOMIC COLLAPSE

An economic collapse is the devastating breakdown of an international, national, or regional economy. It is essentially a severe economic depression characterized by a significant number of businesses going bankrupt and massive unemployment. A complete or nearly complete economic meltdown is often quickly followed by months, years, or even decades of economic depression, social chaos, and civil unrest.

Above: Economic stagnation and, worse, collapse lead to the shuttering of businesses, the loss of jobs, and urban and rural decay as a result.

An economic collapse, however, is much different from an economic disaster resulting from natural causes. For example, when Hurricane Katrina slammed into the Gulf Coast in April 2006, the storm's devastation reached much further than the destruction of homes and property. The hurricane destroyed thirty oil platforms, forced the closure of nine oil refineries, and interrupted the country's oil supply. It also destroyed the Gulf Coast's highway infrastructure and disrupted the export of products, such as grain. Hundreds of thousands of local residents were left unemployed. Thousands of homes were completely submerged in floodwaters that rose 20 to 30 feet (6 to 9 meters) high. Thousands of people were forced to leave New Orleans, Louisiana, and the surrounding areas after the levees broke and flooded the city. Many ended up leaving permanently after discovering that the recovery and rebuilding effort was slow to begin.

However, even amid the wide-scale destruction, the closing of businesses, and the poor response, recovery, and rebuilding effort, the US economy was largely uninterrupted. While people were affected nationally by rising gas prices, the storm did not hurt employment on a national scale. The storm's effects were mostly felt in the Gulf Coast area, which include the states of Texas and Mississippi. The area struggled to recover.

While Hurricane Katrina might represent a regional economic disaster, widespread economic collapse occurs when there are breakdowns in multiple financial and business systems worldwide. These breakdowns cause widespread unemployment, higher rates of interest and inflation, and a considerable slowdown in consumer spending. Often, the government gets involved in bringing the economy back from the brink of collapse. However, government aid can often be slow to arrive.

What Is an Economic Cycle?

Every economy under-goes natural fluctuations over time as the economy grows, then contracts, then grows again. Four basic phases make up an economic cycle:

This illustration shows the variety of emotions people experience as the stock market runs through its regular cycle of ups and downs.

Phase One: *Economic slowdown.* The first phase of the economic cycle begins when the economy begins to slow and the demand for products is not as high.

Phase Two: *Recession.* In this phase, the economy slows to a point where unemployment rises, production slows or stops, and the economy is at its weakest point.

Phase Three: *Economic recovery.* In this phase, the economy is beginning to grow, companies are getting back on track and producing products again, and more jobs become available.

Phase Four: *Expansion.* At this phase, lots of jobs are available, companies are working hard to meet the demand for products, people are investing in businesses, and consumer spending is at its peak.

PAST FINANCIAL DISASTERS

The stock market is a group of exchanges or markets where people can buy and sell stocks and other financial products. Stock is the money that a company raises when it issues shares—small portions of a company's ownership that, when bought by an investor, entitle that investor to a share of the money that the company makes. The health of the stock market is a measure of the health of the economy as a whole. When

A group of unemployed men in New York City line up outside a soup kitchen, waiting for food, during the Great Depression.

the stock market is struggling, businesses are struggling, and when it crashes, businesses and investors alike can lose a great deal of money.

The Great Depression began in 1929 and lasted until about 1939. It was the longest and most severe economic depression ever experienced in the industrialized world. Though the US economy had actually begun to decline six months earlier, the Great Depression began with a stock market crash in October 1929. With the collapse of stock market prices, thousands of individual investors watched their assets, or possessions, decrease in value. The crash strained banks and other financial institutions, particularly those holding stocks in their portfolios. By 1933, of the twenty-five thousand US banks, more than eleven thousand had been forced out of business.

This, combined with a national loss of confidence in the economy, led to lower levels of consumer spending. With no one buying anything beyond the necessities to live each day, there was no longer a need for the great number of products that were available to the public. Manufacturing slowed and many businesses went bankrupt. The result was a drastically increasing unemployment rate. By 1932, US manufacturing production was cut in half and unemployment rose to unprecedented levels of about 25 percent. The United States was not the only country affected, however. The Great Depression was an international economic problem. Countries all around the world were hit hard, especially those dependent on heavy industry.

There have also been several less severe economic recessions since the Great Depression—ones that continue to have lasting effects. Those who worry that another financial meltdown is in our future point out that history tends to repeat itself. It does, indeed.

THE 1987 STOCK MARKET CRASH

The stock market crash of 1987, also known as "Black Monday," refers to a series of international events that occurred on Monday, October 19, 1987. On this date, stock markets around the world crashed, beginning in Hong Kong, spreading through Europe, and finally reaching the United States. Black Monday was the largest one-day decline in the history of the stock market. Heavy stock trading and the overinflated value of stocks were two of the major reasons for the crash.

The most common explanation for the 1987 crash was that investors were program trading, which is the use of computers to perform rapid sales of stock. As computer technology became more widely available, the practice of program trading grew dramatically within Wall Street

The Dow Jones stock index plummeted by more than 200 points on October 19, 1987. A New York Stock Exchange trader reacts to the devastating losses.

firms. After the crash, many Wall Street stockbrokers and financial executives blamed the computer programs for blindly selling stocks as the market continued to fall, which only made the problem worse.

THE SAVINGS AND LOANS COLLAPSE

The savings and loan crisis of the 1980s and 1990s, commonly known as the "S&L crisis," was the failure of 747 savings and loan associations in the United States. The problems began when savings and loan managers created several innovations, such as alternative mortgage instruments and interest-bearing checking accounts, as a way to retain funds and generate loans. This system collapsed when the savings and loans associations did not have enough money on hand when people wanted to withdraw cash from their accounts.

THE "DOT-COM" BUBBLE

Despite the problematic role computers had played in the 1987 crash, their widespread dissemination was inevitable. As the personal computer became more common and the popularity and usefulness of the internet grew, new companies were formed. By 2000, a million new web pages were being created every day.

This was the peak of the "dot-com" bubble, which was formed when countless companies got their big breaks in cyberspace. In economic terms, a bubble is when the price of assets, such as shares, increases rapidly—so rapidly that there is a sudden fall in prices to balance out the overinflated "bubble." Dot-coms, as they were known then, are companies that do the majority of their business on the internet. The bubble burst when a stock market crash in 2000 forced a number of these dot-coms to go out of business. Thousands of people lost their

A man peers through the window of the NASDAQ MarketSite on April 12, 2000, as the NASDAQ was experiencing the second-worst point drop in its history. When the "dot-com" bubble burst, the stock market was devastated.

jobs. Many people who had invested money to help establish these businesses lost some or all of their money.

CAUSES OF THE GREAT RECESSION

The Great Recession, which was discussed in the introduction to this book, was also caused by a bubble—but this time, it was a bubble in the housing market. Between the mid-1990s and the mid-2000s, the average price of a home in the United States increased 124 percent—a rapid increase that created a bubble.

This wasn't the only problem, however. Many banks had lent money to people—in the form of loans called "mortgages"—so that they could buy houses, without making sure that those people would be able to pay the money back. Many banks issued subprime mortgages—that is, mortgages to people with bad credit ratings, meaning that they had little experience managing debt or have managed their debt poorly in the past. Some banks even lent people 100 percent or more of the cost of a home—a practice that was relatively risky, since most home buyers are expected to place a down payment of thousands of dollars of their own money as the initial payment on a house. This down payment gets them started on paying their debt and serves as proof that they have the income and the money-management skills necessary to continue making future payments.

Eventually, there were more homes than there were people who wanted to buy them. Then, there was in increase in the number of foreclosures, in which banks or other institutions reclaimed possession of mortgaged properties whose mortgagors could no longer pay back the money they had borrowed. The housing market crashed, and soon,

Foreclosed homes line Catanzaro Way in Antioch, California, in 2007. The area saw 271 foreclosures between January and August of 2007, during the US subprime mortgage crisis that contributed to the Great Recession.

financial products that were based on the health of these subprime mortgages also plummeted in value. Many of these products, often called mortgage-backed securities, had been packaged in such a way that the investors and banks that bought them did not realize just how risky they were.

At the same time as the value of people's homes were dropping, many were being asked to pay higher monthly bills, which caused further economic stagnation. Meanwhile, the purchase of risky financial products caused many investment banks to pursue bankruptcy proceedings—only to be bailed out by the US government. In 2018, some were warning that another housing bubble was underway—or, at least, that home prices would soon decrease again. As editor Brad Finkelstein wrote in the *National Mortgage News* in March 2018, "It's simply the nature of a cyclical market."

CHAPTER 2

CAUSES OF A FINANCIAL MELTDOWN

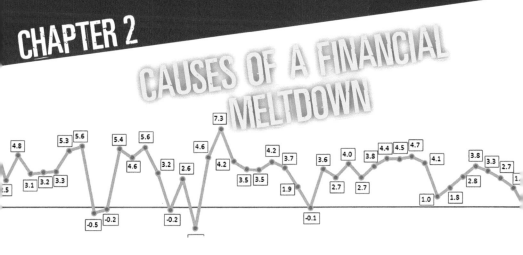

Big banks making poor investments is just one possible cause of a financial collapse. Bank runs can lead to such a meltdown, but such runs can be provoked by a number of different events. An internet virus that prevents financial transactions or communication could paralyze financial markets. As the number of cyberattacks and cases of identity theft grow, more people's money is at risk all the time, and a massive financial theft orchestrated by a hacker or hackers is also possible. If a war or widespread violence were to break out, or if a terrorist attack knocked out communication or transportation systems, this could prevent the US government from quickly responding to a financial collapse as it did in 2008. And if the value of the US dollar were to drop, the price of goods might skyrocket, and many people might reinvest in different currencies, such as the euro, gold, or even cryptocurrencies such as Bitcoin. US and global financial markets are connected, and problems in one large market can wreak havoc around the world. All of these scenarios—and many others—could lead to a financial meltdown.

Above: US economic growth, shown as historical GDP growth, has varied widely between 1961 and 2015.

This chapter will examine four of the most likely such scenarios: a massive economic crash, the widespread global use of cryptocurrencies, the influence and impact that the country of China has on the United States, and the threat of another major terrorist attack on the United States.

AN ECONOMIC CRASH

The likeliest of all scenarios is an economic crash—mostly because such events have happened before. An economic crash is characterized by rampant deflation, which is the lowering of prices over time; 15 percent unemployment; and a 35 percent loss of gross domestic product (GDP). GDP is one of the ways we measure a country's national income and

A Lehman Brothers employee carries a box of his things away from the company's New York City headquarters on September 15, 2008, after it filed a bankruptcy petition.

its economy. GDP is the total value of all the goods and services produced in a particular country. The United States has the highest GDP worldwide, followed by China, Japan, Germany, and the United Kingdom, respectively, according to the International Monetary Fund's April 2018 "World Economic Outlook."

Can an economic crash occur? It can, and it has. The Great Depression was the most severe economic crash in world history. Many experts say that a crash of that magnitude is not likely to occur again. However, severe economic crashes will happen as a result of the natural highs and lows of the economy. The most damaging in recent years was the Great Recession of 2007–2009. There have been other such incidents since, however. Nearly 70 percent of investors in the United States lost money in 2015; many called it the worst stock year since 2008. A drop in stock prices in early 2016 sent some countries into recession; investors lost trillions of dollars.

ALTERNATIVE CURRENCIES

There are more than 190 different currencies, or types of money, in the world. Every country has its own currency: Switzerland has the franc; England has the pound; Japan has the yen; China has the yuan. Most European countries have a shared form of currency called the euro, which was introduced in 1999. However, the prevailing currency worldwide is the US dollar. The dollar is the major international reserve currency, which is a form of money that is held in significant quantities by many governments and institutions throughout the world.

In recent years, a number of cryptocurrencies have emerged, including Ripple and Ethereum. A cryptocurrency is used like cash money is used—to pay for goods and services—but it is exchanged

Bitcoin is one of many cryptocurrencies that have emerged in recent years. Some believe such currencies could threaten the stability of financial markets.

digitally. Encryption is used to regulate the currency and to transfer funds. Central banks, national banks associated with a country's government, are generally responsible for implementing monetary policy in that country. Cryptocurrencies, however, don't rely upon and are not regulated by central banks. Bitcoin, one of the earliest and most commonly traded cryptocurrencies, appeared in 2009; who created it remains a mystery. Many worry that cryptocurrencies are being used to commit financial crimes.

However, as more investors become interested in cryptocurrencies, they might become more directly linked with traditional financial markets—and that could threaten the stability of those markets, warns Garrick Hileman, a University of Cambridge economic historian. Being able to quickly and easily leave a struggling financial market and instead invest one's money in an unconnected market, such as a cryptocurrency, may make it more likely that investors will do so in times of crisis—which could make the crisis worse. Meanwhile, because there isn't yet much reliable information about cryptocurrency markets, scams are more likely to dupe investors.

Many experts—including Iwa Salami, a senior lecturer in financial law and regulation at the University of East London—have argued that governmental regulation is necessary for avoiding a financial crisis. Like Hileman, Salami has pointed out that cryptocurrencies could trigger a crisis if "enough systemically important financial institutions … hold and trade them when a downturn occurs." One of the risks is among businesses that seek to raise money on cryptocurrency markets. Because the same regulations do not apply in such markets as in traditional markets, such businesses are not required to prove the value of their product or service in the same way, meaning investors are less protected. Another risk, according to Salami, is that there may be a bubble among such currencies. Many point to the high price of bitcoin in December 2017 as such a bubble. If enough people own a cryptocurrency when such a bubble bursts, a crisis could be triggered.

Ken Rogoff, a former chief economist at the International Monetary Fund, predicted in 2018 that cryptocurrencies wouldn't remain unregulated by governmental entities for long—despite the fact many supporters of such currencies like them precisely because of this independence from governmental regulation. "We have to remember the private sector invented standardized coinage, and then the government eventually regulated it, took it over," he told *Business Insider.* "I'm sorry[,] when it comes to the monetary system, the government makes the rules. You cannot win the game. If they're not winning, they will change the rules. That's what will happen here."

The Centre for Macroeconomics, a United Kingdom–based research organization, published a survey in December 2017 in which most economists did not believe that cryptocurrencies posed a very big risk to traditional markets yet—they were still "too small and too detached from other financial markets." Just about 20 percent said that they were a threat or would "become a threat in the next couple of years." Hileman warned, though, that changes were happening very quickly; he pointed to the meteoric rise in the price of bitcoin in 2017. (Its price dropped in early 2018.)

On March 22, 2018, US president Donald Trump holds up a memorandum he has signed announcing tariffs on up to $60 billion in Chinese goods.

Among those who don't want to bank on the value of the US dollar, gold is another popular alternative. Gold used to be a form of currency, but that changed once countries began to adopt paper currency, such as the American dollar. Then gold became an investment. However, in times of financial crisis, when paper currency decreases in value, gold maintains or increases its value.

CHINESE TRADE AND GROWTH

There is an urban legend spreading that talks about the chances of a United States–China war. The story goes like this: while working for an international corporation, experts on China uncover information about how it intends to launch an attack on the United States. The attack will begin with the Chinese military launching missiles on American military bases in Japan and South Korea, while also launching long-range weapons to destroy American satellites in order to cause a disruption of communications.

In reality, this wartime scenario is pretty far-fetched. However, China does have major influence over the US financial system, and that could spell big trouble for the United States. At the same time, China relies on the American dollar to fuel its own economy. China's growth as a country relies on its sales of goods and services to other countries. Its economy is the second-largest in the world after that of the United States, and the United States is very much at the mercy of China when it comes to prices, wages, interest rates, and the value of the American dollar.

This economic interdependency was challenged in early 2018, when many experts warned that a newly instigated trade war with China could hurt both the US and Chinese economies. US president Donald Trump had imposed tariffs—taxes on imported goods—on steel and aluminum from China. In retaliation, China instituted tariffs on nearly 130 US goods, including food products such as pork. Such tariffs reduce the income of American farmers and other producers of these exported goods—and likewise hurt Chinese workers responsible for producing steel and other products exported to the United States. Still, experts predicted that the trade war might continue to escalate. The *Washington Post* reported in April 2018 that these tariffs were "unlikely to damage the overall economy significantly, but it's getting to the point where American consumers are likely to face higher prices on televisions, shoes, clothes and possibly even iPhones." A report from the Brookings Institution, a nonprofit public-policy organization, found that, should China institute all the tariffs it had threatened as of early April, about 2.1 million American jobs would be impacted.

Economics reporter Patrick W. Watson, writing for *Forbes* in April 2018, pointed out that China buys so many US Treasury securities that "China is our government's largest foreign lender." In instituting these new tariffs, President Trump was in part seeking to reduce the United States' trade deficit with China—the amount that Americans spend on Chinese goods compared with the lesser amount the Chinese spend on American goods. However, if this deficit is reduced, Watson warns that China might buy fewer US Treasury bonds, which could make it harder for the United States to manage its debt and may make that debt more expensive. This can have huge, negative ripple effects on the US and global economies.

China may face other economic challenges in the years ahead. In 2018, Rogoff told *Business Insider* that the likelihood of a financial crisis was "[l]ow—I mean outside of China—if one's going to happen it's in China." China had seen a great deal of growth in recent years,

The 2008 Economic Stimulus Act

In February 2008, the US Congress passed the Economic Stimulus Act to institute several measures intended to motivate the economy, boosting it before it sank further into a recession, or even a depression.

The stimulus package included tax rebates to low-income and middle-income taxpayers; tax incentives to stimulate business investment; the expansion of unemployment benefits and other social welfare provisions; an increase in domestic spending in such areas as education, health care, and infrastructure (roads, highways, bridges, etc.); and an investment in the energy industry. Experts disagree as to how effective this legislation was in helping the US economy recover from the Great Recession.

Omega Mckenzie worked for Merrill Lynch, a wealth-management **bank** division, for thirteen years, but lost her job as a result of the September 11, 2001, terrorist attacks. Here, she stands outside an unemployment office.

and housing prices were up. Debt was also up. "I tend to think they could have trouble maintaining their growth without some kind of big bump," Rogoff said. And because global markets are interconnected, any downturn in China could have global ripple effects.

TERRORISM AND THE ECONOMY

Terrorist attacks can influence the economy. In places where terrorist activity has, in the past, been pervasive and protracted—such as Colombia, Northern Ireland, and Israel—terrorism depresses growth and sometimes stunts economic development. Foreign companies and the money that they would have invested fled Colombia long ago because the country was beset by drug-related terrorism for decades. The per-capita income level for this Latin American nation in the years before FARC, a dominant guerrilla organization there, instigated peace talks with the government in 2012 was roughly 45 percent below the global average. Similarly, when religious violence raged through Belfast in the 1980s and early 1990s, Northern Ireland became the United Kingdom's poorest region as industry and people migrated to the southern republic to escape the terrorist attacks and live in a more secure location.

Al-Qaeda, the terrorist organization responsible for the attacks on the World Trade Center and the Pentagon on September 11, 2001, has long sought to disrupt the US economy. The 9/11 attacks influenced every sector of the American economy. In the days and weeks that followed the attacks, retail sales and travel dropped to significantly lower levels. The financial market also struggled to regain its footing. It took several months for these areas of the economy to rebound—but slowly, they did. Retail sales improved, and while the stock market was hit hard immediately after the attacks, it rebounded to pre–9/11 levels within just a few of months.

Terrorist attacks not only cause a loss of human life and often devastating destruction, as witnessed by the collapse of the World Trade Center in New York City; they also generate widespread fear. Terrorist attacks create a general feeling that we are not safe and perpetuate the fear that more violence is to come. This fear can influence the way that people invest their money, as uncertainty can make people hesitant to invest and can hurt business growth. In addition, the fear of violence often forces companies to spend more money on security. After the 9/11 attacks, many businesses hired more security guards, strengthened their computer security by establishing better firewalls, invested in storage for company records and important paperwork, and took out large insurance policies. This widespread investment in safety took money away from more productive investments, such as employees.

These are just a few of the scenarios that could cause a financial meltdown. However, as economists discovered with the collapse of the housing bubble in 2007, financial meltdowns can be hard to foresee. Countless complex factors contribute to the ebb and swell of the economy, and it can be difficult to predict which factors will be most integral to local and global financial health.

CHAPTER 3
THREE WORST-CASE SCENARIOS

When you consider just how much can go wrong, it can become far too easy to imagine scenarios in which the worst possible consequences of a financial meltdown come to pass: all commerce shuts down; people are left homeless and starving; unemployment soars. However, examining these worse-case scenarios more closely allows us to consider what is really likely to happen, and to judge whether each situation is a valid potential threat. In this chapter, we will consider three such scenarios: a sweeping depression; a war between the United States and China; and a terrorist attack.

A FULL-SCALE DEPRESSION

Robert Parks, an economist and finance professor at Pace University in New York City, predicted that there was a more than 60 percent probability that financial meltdown in the United States in 2008 would lead to a full-scale depression, much like the Great Depression of the 1930s. Parks believed there would be a steep fall in housing prices, major deficits in the federal budget, a continual decrease in the value of the American dollar, and a weak stock market. He believed these factors would lead to a depression in which the United States would

Above: An impoverished mother of seven is photographed with her children during the height of the Great Depression in the 1930s.

see widespread poverty, rampant foreclosures, unemployment, and even starvation. While Parks was right in guessing that there would be a significant economic crisis in 2008, he was wrong about how severe it would become.

Many economists and financial experts thought Parks was wrong. The Great Depression was far worse than the Great Repression in a number of ways. During the Great Depression, the unemployment rate rose to as high as 25 percent, compared to 10 percent at the height of the Great Recession. The average family's income dropped by 40 percent during the Great Depression, compared to 17 percent during the Great Recession. Here are a few other economic changes that the United States underwent during the Great Depression, which lasted more than a decade:

- Industrial production dropped by 45 percent.
- New home building dropped by 80 percent.
- The stock market lost nearly 90 percent of its value.
- More than one million families lost their farms.
- Nine million savings accounts were wiped out.
- Many people, because they were unable to earn an income, went hungry.

The US government, in response to the declining economy in 2008 and at the start of 2009, proposed solutions to help it get back on its feet. The federal government assisted banks through bailouts, in which the government gave banks money to help cover their debts and loans. A highly detailed infrastructure plan was put into place to improve schools, highways and roads, bridges, and public buildings—much like a plan called the New Deal that was instituted to fight the Great Depression. The goal was to create new construction jobs, which would in turn stimulate the economy because people could feel more secure in their personal financial health and could begin to spend money again. The plan had mixed results, as individuals remained hesitant to spend or invest as much as they once had for several years afterward. The stock market hit record highs and key milestones in 2017 and 2018, leading some to worry that another bubble was underway—or, at least, that a "market correction" that would drop these prices was long overdue.

A WAR BETWEEN CHINA AND THE UNITED STATES

Jed Babbin's 2006 book, *Showdown: Why China Wants War with the United States*, argued that China was looking to pick a fight with the United States. Showdown predicted the ways in which a war between the two nations, including the potential for China to wage a nuclear attack on the United States or engage in cyberwarfare, and China's growing economic clout and obsession with oil-rich nations, which could upset the Unites States' supply of oil. Some of these scenarios are much more likely to occur than others; most experts don't consider nuclear war very likely at this time. On the other hand, by 2018 there was significant evidence that state-sponsored Chinese hackers have launched cyberattacks on US companies, especially for the purpose of unearthing trade secrets.

China's push for superpower status on a world stage long dominated by the United States may be a key factor in provoking hostilities between the two nations. In 2017, Graham Allison, a professor of government at

Chinese president Xi Jinping (*left*) and US president Donald Trump (*right*) have butted heads over tariffs and trade in 2018. The conflict could affect the economic health of both countries.

Harvard University, wrote, "When a rising power threatens to displace a ruling power, alarm bells should sound: danger ahead. China and the United States are currently on a collision course for war—unless both parties take difficult and painful actions to avert it." In particular, Allison pointed to the personalities of the countries' two leaders in 2018 as potential points of friction. "If Hollywood were making a movie pitting China against the United States on the path to war, central casting could not find two better leading actors than Xi Jinping and Donald Trump," he wrote. Both identified the other nation as a key obstacle in their goal to increase their countries' global influence.

Similarly, in February 2018, US Navy admiral Harry Harris warned Congress that China's policy of military expansionism, especially in the South China Sea, means the United States must be prepared for a possible war. China had built military bases on seven islands in the region that were in fact disputed territory. "China's impressive military build-up could soon challenge the United States across almost every domain," Harris argued. "I'm hopeful that it won't come to a conflict with China, but we must all be prepared for that if it should come to that."

China's growing economy is a factor that definitely deserves attention. With its low labor standards, the country has taken jobs away from the United States and has exported its products overseas at what some say are unfairly low prices. In truth, the jobs that China has taken away from US workers are generally designed for an unskilled and uneducated workforce. They are mostly seen as jobs that the American workforce is uninterested in doing. Also, a large percentage of Chinese exports to the United States are produced by firms owned by foreign companies, many of them American. These companies have moved their operations overseas in order to lower production costs, which in turn lowers prices for consumers. Meanwhile, the United States has a number of very large, very powerful companies that import goods from China. These companies, including Walmart and Hallmark, have the power to force Chinese suppliers to keep their costs as low as possible. Walmart, which is the biggest importer in the United States, brought in $49 billion in Chinese goods in 2013. The Economic Policy Institute has estimated that, between 2001 and 2013, more than four hundred thousand US jobs were displaced or eliminated as a result of Walmart's imports from China. Most of the jobs were in manufacturing.

A war between China and the United States is pretty unlikely. Many argue that the countries are too dependent on each other economically to let this happen. However, many experts are keeping a cautious eye on the situation.

Financial Crisis in Film

Best Picture

THE BIG SHORT

The Big Short, an award-winning film, depicted the factors contributing to the Great Recession.

Hollywood, California, one of the moviemaking capitals of the world, has released a number of films that critique questionable financial practices and investigate how some of the world's biggest financial crises have come to pass. Among these was *The Big Short* (2015), which won an Academy Award for Best Writing, Adapted Screenplay, and was nominated in four other categories. This dramatic comedy investigated the shady financial dealings that led to the Great Recession. *Wall Street* (1987) critiqued the famously greedy and unscrupulous practices of stockbrokers during the 1980s and was released the same year as a massive stock market crash. *The Wolf of Wall Street* (2013), starring Leonardo DiCaprio, tackled similar themes.

TERRORISTS ATTACK

Terrorism is any act that is intended to create fear in a deliberate target. On September 11, 2001, a terrorist organization attacked the United States. Over the course of just a few hours, there was a massive loss of life, significant disruption to the US financial system, and widespread fear. Terrorism can come in many forms. There is political, religious, and civil terrorism—and there is a fourth type of terrorism that is on the rise: cyberterrorism.

Cyberterrorism is the use of computers and the global interconnectivity afforded by the internet to cause physical harm or the severe disruption of infrastructure. Terrorists could target computer networks that are critical to a nation's power supplies, telecommunications, and financial systems, and thereby wreak substantial havoc.

The threat of cyberterrorism has grabbed the attention of the mass media, the security community, and the computer and information technology industry. Journalists, politicians, and experts in a variety of fields have envisioned elaborate scenarios in which sophisticated cyberterrorists hack into computers and gain control of our government, military, air traffic control, and financial systems to endanger the lives of thousands—even millions—of people while creating a massive national security risk.

The potential threat of a cyberterrorist attack is terrifying. While no act of cyberterrorism has yet been known to cause loss of life, cyberattacks may have already put lives at risk. For example, in 2017, a piece of ransomware called WannaCry disrupted the computer and telephone systems of approximately one hundred thousand organizations around the world—including those belonging to the National Health Service in the United Kingdom. The virus demanded that the NHS and

Cyberterrorists may have the ability to hack into and **disable large and powerful** institutions, including banks and financial institutions. **However, many types of** cyberattacks have the potential to cause a financial **crisis.**

other affected organizations pay a ransom in order to regain access to their computers. Such an attack could leave medical personnel without access to key information about patients and their medical histories, which can in turn put patients in danger. Likewise, telephone network disruptions could prevent people from contacting emergency services. Meanwhile, another computer virus, Stuxnet, has damaged equipment in the physical world. How much more difficult would it be, then, to make such damage to infrastructure more widespread, and more dangerous to humans?

CHAPTER 4
HOW TO PREVENT A MELTDOWN

Bail Out the People

The economy will inevitably grow and shrink as part of its natural cycle. Worst-case scenarios may make a financial meltdown seem unavoidable, but there are a number of strategies and policies that can avert a true crisis. Let's take a look at what is being done to ensure that these financial doomsday scenarios never come to pass.

BAILOUTS

When the financial services industry has faced severe problems in the past, the US government has often provided the industry with bailouts to help steady the economy before a major collapse could occur—as it did in 2008, during the Great Recession. A bailout is when a government loans or gives money to a failing business to save it from bankruptcy or collapse. The federal government has been bailing out companies for decades to keep people employed and avoid economic crisis. In the 1970s, it gave a substantial financial life raft to Lockheed, a company engaged in the research, development, and manufacture of advanced technology systems, products, and services. The company's failure would have meant significant job loss for the people of California, where

Above: Demonstrators outside the New York Stock Exchange in 2008 protest the government bailout package offered to big banks during the Great Recession.

FedEx was one of the companies to receive compensation under the Air Transportation Safety and Stabilization Act for their financial loss after the 9/11 attacks. FedEx later challenged an order to repay some of the money.

the company was headquartered, as well as a significant impact on America's national defense.

Similarly, the federal government stepped in when the 9/11 terrorist attacks crippled the US airline industry, which was already financially troubled. After the attacks, the government grounded all airlines until it could determine exactly what had happened. Grounding the airlines caused massive financial strain on the industry, so Congress enacted the Air Transportation Safety and Stabilization Act. The law compensated airlines for their financial loss and was intended to keep the industry afloat in a time when people were afraid of flying.

Some financial experts are concerned that, when the government moves to bail out ailing companies or industries, it is really keeping the financial crisis from reaching rock bottom, and in fact delaying the

economy's natural recovery process. Others believe that government bailouts are necessary to help the economy calm down and help assets stabilize in value. When the economy is unhinged, people don't know the real value of their assets and what investment banks are actually worth. This can cause economic paralysis, in which people are too fearful to spend any money, thus creating economic stagnation. Government bailouts help motivate the economy and create a sense of calm that encourages people to spend money, thus boosting the economy. In addition to the airline industry, the federal government has bailed out banks, the auto industry, the financial services industry, and even the city of New York when it fell on hard times.

SHIFTS IN CONSUMER BEHAVIOR

In the case of financial crisis, most Americans would likely make an effort to find cheaper prices for the products they buy. Likewise, they might spend less on nonessentials, such as entertainment, recreation, and eating at restaurants. After the Great Recession, more Americans

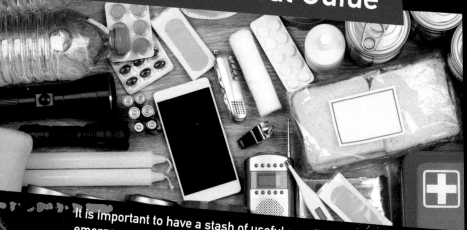

A Personal Survival Guide

It is important to have a stash of useful supplies in case of an emergency such as a financial meltdown.

In order to prepare for a global financial meltdown, keep cash on hand. In the case of a bank failure, you'll be in serious trouble if you have more in the bank than the government insures. In an absolute worst-case scenario, cash could become worthless—but in most cases, it will save you.

Stockpile nonperishable food. A major meltdown to our financial system, a terrorist attack, or a cyberattack could mean the disruption of power supplies, which would spoil perishable foods. Transportation systems could also be interrupted, meaning stores could run out of food.

Financial advisors recommend keeping a minimum of three to six months' worth of living expenses in the bank in case you lose your job. In the event of a major financial collapse, your job could be at risk. Extra savings will enable you to pay your mortgage or rent, food, utilities, and other essential expenses.

When people are struggling to pay for basic needs, they might use coupons or other tactics to spend less overall, which can hurt the economy.

focused on building their savings accounts and reducing their debt. In short, during financial crises, consumer behavior changes.

Such changes affect more than just the US financial system. Goods and services purchased by Americans make up a significant percentage of the global economy. When the economy is healthy, Americans buy more goods and services. That translates into jobs and economic growth around the world. However, when the economy is faring badly, spending decreases as a result, and economies around the world feel the pinch.

When a financial crisis strikes, retailers are among the first to feel the immediate aftershocks. When people begin to struggle to pay their credit cards, basic household expenses, and mortgages, spending on new plasma-screen televisions, cars, and expensive clothes declines.

President Barack Obama signs the Dodd-Frank Wall Street **Reform and** Consumer Protection Act in 2010. The goal of the legislation was **to rein in the** banks so as to prevent another event like the Great Recession.

However, any purchases, even the small ones—such as DVDs, movie tickets, and dinner out—help keep the economy moving.

NEW FINANCIAL REGULATIONS

In 2008, the financial industry nearly collapsed under the weight of deregulation imposed a decade earlier. Among the widespread abuses committed by banks were off-the-books accounting to hide losses and debt; offering investment, commercial banking, and insurance services that proved to be a conflict of interest; and loaning to those who were not able to pay the money back.

Another problem was that banks and other financial institutions were not required to be open and honest to the government about what they were doing and how bad their debt really was. Because the US financial system is global—meaning that American banks do business with British, Chinese, Japanese, and other banks around the world—the United States was forced to lead an international effort to find out where these bad investments are in other nations' banks. Understanding the full scale of the problem was the only way to find regulations that worked for both the US financial system and the global marketplace.

As a result of the Great Recession, new regulations were put in place. The Dodd-Frank Wall Street Reform and Consumer Protection Act, passed in 2010, instituted more than two hundred new rules designed to rein in the banks that had been bailed out two years before. It established several governmental oversight agencies, including the Consumer Financial Protection Bureau (CFPB), which was designed to investigate questionable practices in the financial sector. The Financial Stability Oversight Council was tasked with monitoring the stability of major financial companies, and was given the power to break apart banks that might be "too big to fail," as was the case in the 2008 bailout. And, significantly, Dodd-Frank limited risky investments and trading practices, and required that banks hold more of their assets in cash, limiting the amount of money they could have invested at any one time.

Cybersecurity measures play a key role in protecting the economic stability and financial security of institutions, governments, and nations.

Opponents to Dodd-Frank have argued that restricting banks' abilities to make risky investments also unduly limits their profit potential, and in turn suppresses economic growth. In 2018, Congress was chipping away at provisions of the law. Some argued this would put the economy at risk of another crisis like the Great Recession.

CYBERSECURITY

"There is no such thing as a totally secure system," says Kevin Mitnick, one of the world's most famous hackers. Mitnick spent nearly five years in jail for seven software felonies involving hacking. "All it takes is one vulnerability to compromise an entire system," Mitnick explains.

Avoiding these vulnerabilities is the job of cybersecurity firms. Many financial institutions provide electronic connectivity from their networks to payment networks like Fedwire. Fedwire is a money transfer system set up by the Federal Reserve Bank.

These connections pose a great risk. Major financial institutions such as Wells Fargo often have the most secure, up-to-date software and security programs available. Therefore, it is often much easier for hackers to target small, local banks that might work with Fedwire. Smaller banks might not have extensive computer security systems that monitor network security. This makes it possible for hackers to gain access to the system through the internet, gain administrative control of an inside computer with access to one of these payment networks, and launch the attack. Even so, large financial institutions such as Citibank have indeed been hacked, and the personal identity data of their customers has been compromised.

With cyberterrorism becoming more of a potential threat, President Barack Obama created a new position, unofficially called the "cyber-czar," in 2009. In a 2017 executive order, President Donald Trump called for federal agencies to carefully assess the security of their computer systems, and insisted that more educational resources needed to be dedicated to training cybersecurity experts; there was projected to be a shortage of 1.8 million workers in this field by 2022.

Economic downturns are inevitable. Every boom must end, but luckily, crises too have an expiration date. Responsible regulation and business practices can ensure that downturns don't turn into meltdowns, and that businesses and individuals alike have the chance to succeed in an economic environment built to sustain and protect everyone.

GLOSSARY

asset An item of value, such as a home, stock, or investment.

bailout Monetary aid from the federal government given to banks and other institutions to help these institutions cover their loans, debts, and other costs of operation.

Bitcoin A digital cryptocurrency created in 2009.

bubble In economic terms, a situation in which the price of assets, such as shares, increases so rapidly that it results in a sudden market correction in the form of a price drop that balances or corrects it.

cryptocurrency A digital currency that is used to pay for goods and services, but that it is only exchanged digitally. Encryption is used to regulate the currency and to transfer funds.

dollar The currency of the United States; issued by the US Federal Reserve, it is the most traded currency in the world.

encryption The process of transforming information to make it unreadable.

euro The currency of the European Union; introduced to the global financial market in 1999.

free market An economic system in which competition between businesses is unrestricted.

gross domestic product (GDP) A measure of national income and output for a given country's economy; the total value of all final goods and services produced in a particular economy.

guerrilla Referring to the activities or members of an independent group that engages in irregular or disorganized fighting, often in opposition to larger military forces.

inflation A rise in the general level of prices of goods and services in an economy over a period of time.

interest rate The price that a borrower pays for the use of money that he or she does not own.

levee An embankment constructed to prevent a body of water from overflowing.

manufacturing The use of machines, tools, and labor to make things for use or sale.

network A group of interconnected computers.

overinflated Exaggerated; excessive.

portfolio A mixture of investments held by either a financial institution or a private citizen.

program trading The use of computers to perform rapid sales of stock.

ransomware A type of malware that requires a victim to pay a ransom in exchange for restoring their access to encrypted files.

share Partial ownership of a publicly traded company.

stagnation Lack of growth, development, or activity.

stock The money that a company raises when it issues shares.

tariff A duty or tax on imported or exported goods.

Wall Street A neighborhood, located in New York City, that forms the center of the US financial services industry.

FURTHER INFORMATION

BOOKS

Burkholder, Steve. *I Want More Pizza: Real World Money Skills for High School, College, and Beyond*. Edited by Rebecca Maizel and David Aretha. Encinitas, CA: Overcome Publishing LLC, 2017.

El-Erian, Mohamed A. *The Only Game in Town: Central Banks, Instability, and Avoiding the Next Collapse*. New York: Random House, 2016.

King, Mervyn. *The End of Alchemy: Money, Banking, and the Future of the Global Economy*. New York: W. W. Norton & Company, Inc., 2016.

Varoufakis, Yanis. *Talking to My Daughter About the Economy: or, How Capitalism Works—and How It Fails*. Translated by Jacob Moe and Yanis Varoufakis. New York: Farrar, Straus and Giroux, 2018.

WEBSITES

The Balance

https://www.thebalance.com
This website features articles about personal finance and money management written by experts.

Investopedia

https://www.investopedia.com
Billing itself as "the largest financial education website in the world," Investopedia offers definitions of essential finance- and money-related terms and explanations of complicated concepts, legislation, and financial events.

The Mint

http://www.themint.org
This site offers tips for teens on financial literacy, spending, saving, investing, and earning money.

VIDEOS

The Big Short

https://www.imdb.com/title/tt1596363/?ref_=ttawd_awd_tt

This award-winning film is a fictionalized depiction of the real-life events that led to the Great Recession of 2007–2009.

How to Spot a Financial Crisis Before It Spots You

https://www.youtube.com/watch?v=MKQZYs8qREs
In this explanatory video from the Financial Times, economist David McWilliams explains how the next financial meltdown can be prevented.

Warren Buffett's Secret Millionaires Club

http://www.smckids.com
This animated web series offers financial tips from Warren Buffett, one of the most successful investors of all time.

ORGANIZATIONS

Consumer Financial Protection Bureau

P.O. Box 2900
Clinton, IA 52733-2900
(855) 411-2372
https://www.consumerfinance.gov
This federal agency, instituted in 2010, is tasked with protecting consumers from unfair and deceptive business practices in the financial sector.

Financial Consumer Agency of Canada

427 Laurier Avenue West, 6th Floor
Ottawa ON K1R 1B9
(866) 461-3222
https://www.canada.ca/en/financial-consumer-agency.html
This organization seeks to protect Canadian consumers by ensuring that the financial sector complies with federal regulations and educating the public on financial matters.

Harvard Business School

Soldier's Field
Boston, MA 02163
(617) 495-6000
http://www.hbs.edu
This is one of the leading business schools in the world.

National Center on Education and the Economy

2121 K Street NW, Suite 700
Washington, DC 20037
(202) 379-1800
http://ncee.org
This organization funds and publishes research on how the state of the international economy impacts American education.

National Endowment for Financial Education

1331 17th Street, Suite 1200
Denver, CO 80202
(303) 741-6333
https://www.nefe.org
NEFE is a nonprofit foundation that seeks to guide and educate individuals and families in their financial decision-making.

Organisation for Economic Co-operation and Development

2, rue André Pascal
75775 Paris Cedex 16
France
+33 1 45 24 82 00
https://www.oecd.org
The OECD is a forum enabling the cooperation of governments and organizations with the goal of improving the economic wellbeing of people around the globe.

Prosper Canada

60 St. Clair Avenue East, Suite 700
Toronto, Ontario M4T 1N5
(416) 665-2828
http://prospercanada.org
This charity organization, which aims to fight poverty and expand economic opportunity throughout Canada, offers coaching and guidance on financial literacy.

BIBLIOGRAPHY

Allison, Graham. "War between China and the United States Isn't Inevitable, but It's Likely: An Excerpt from Graham Allison's *Destined for War.*" *National Post* (Canada), March 5, 2018. http://nationalpost.com/opinion/war-between-china-and-the-united-states-isnt-inevitable-but-its-likely-an-excerpt-from-graham-allisons-destined-for-war.

Amadeo, Kimberly. "Are We Headed for Another Great Depression?" *Balance*, March 24, 2018. https://www.thebalance.com/could-the-great-depression-happen-again-3305685.

———. "Dow Highest Closing Records." *Balance*, April 5, 2018. https://www.thebalance.com/dow-jones-closing-history-top-highs-and-lows-since-1929-3306174.

———. "Treasury Bills, Notes, and Bonds with Examples of How They Work." *Balance*, January 15, 2018. https://www.thebalance.com/what-are-treasury-bills-notes-and-bonds-3305609.

———. "Reserve Primary Fund: It Broke the Buck, Causing a Money Market Run." *Balance*, April 18, 2017. https://www.thebalance.com/reserve-primary-fund-3305671.

———. "U.S. Debt Default Causes and Consequences." *Balance*, December 4, 2017. https://www.thebalance.com/u-s-debt-default-3306295.

———. "U.S. Economy Collapse: What Will Happen, How to Prepare." *Balance*, January 26, 2018. https://www.thebalance.com/u-s-economy-collapse-what-will-happen-how-to-prepare-3305690.

———. "What Was Obama's Stimulus Package?" *Balance*, January 1, 2018. https://www.thebalance.com/what-was-obama-s-stimulus-package-3305625.

"Bailout Recipients." *ProPublica*, April 17, 2018. https://projects. propublica.org/bailout/list.

"Basic Tips on Surviving a Global Financial Meltdown." Inquisitir, September 25, 2008. http://www.inquisitr.com/3935/basic-tips-on-surviving-a-global-financial-meltdown.

"Bitcoin and the City." Centre for Macroeconomics, CFM Surveys, December 19, 2017. http://cfmsurvey.org/surveys/bitcoin-and-city.

Boykin, Ryan. "The Great Recession's Impact on the Housing Market." *Investopedia*, October 13, 2017. https://www. investopedia.com/investing/great-recessions-impact-housing-market.

"China Makes U.S. Economy Its Hostage." *Pravda*, October 10, 2007. http://english.pravda.ru/business/finance/99414-0.

Collins, Keith. "What You Need to Know About Trump's Executive Order on Cybersecurity." *Quartz*, May 12, 2017. https:// qz.com/982128/what-you-need-to-know-about-trumps-executive-order-on-cybersecurity.

Colvin, Geoff. "The Anti-Doomsday Scenario." CNN, June 25, 2008. http://money.cnn.com/200806/24/news/economy/colvin_recovery.fortune/index.htm.

"Dodd-Frank Wall Street Reform and Consumer Protection Act." *Investopedia*. Accessed May 3, 2018. https://www.investopedia.com/terms/d/dodd-frank-financial-regulatory-reform-bill.asp.

Doherty, Ben. "Admiral Warns US Must Prepare for Possibility of War with China." *Guardian* (UK), February 16, 2018. https:// www.theguardian.com/world/2018/feb/16/admiral-warns-us-must-prepare-for-possibility-of-war-with-china.

"Doomsday Fears of Terror Cyber-attacks." BBC News, October 11, 2001. http://news.bbc.co.uk/1/hi/sci/tech/1593018.stm.

Finkelstein, Brad. "Housing Bubble or Not, the Real Estate Market Is in Trouble." *National Mortgage News*, March 28, 2018. https://www.nationalmortgagenews.com/news/housing-bubble-or-not-the-real-estate-market-is-in-trouble.

"4 Financial Doomsday Scenarios." *Newser*, December 17, 2008. http://www.newser.com/story/45591/4-financial-dooms-day-scenarios.html.

Francis, David R. "Recession Is a Given. Can We Avoid Depression?" *Christian Science Monitor*, March 24, 2008. http://www.csmonitor.com/2008/0324/p17s02-wmgn.html?page=10.

Gaffen, David. "Betting Against the Doomsday Scenario." *Wall Street Journal*, January 30, 2009. http://blogs.wsj.com/marketbeat/2009/01/30/betting-against-the-doomsday-scenario.

Hawver, Joe. "Global Financial Meltdown Is a Simple Matter of Information Asymmetry." MLive.com, January 5, 2009. http://www.mlive.com/opinion/kalamazoo/index.ssf/2009/01/global_financial_meltdown_is_a.html.

Hodgson, Camilla. "Bitcoin Could Trigger the Next Financial Crisis." *Business Insider*, December 22, 2017. http://www.businessinsider.com/bitcoin-could-trigger-financial-crisis-2017-12.

Long, Heather. "In a U.S.-China Trade War, Who Has More to Lose?" *Washington Post*, April 5, 2018. https://www.washingtonpost.com/news/wonk/wp/2018/04/05/china-has-more-to-lose-in-a-trade-war-but-trump-has-a-key-weakness/?utm_term=.90e7d5a0efae.

Michaels, Adrian. "This Financial Crisis Is Now Truly Global." *Telegraph* (UK), February 20, 2009. http://www.telegraph.co.uk/finance/financetopics/financialcrisis/4736387/This-financial-crisis-is-now-truly-global.html.

Nakajima, Makoto. "The Diverse Impacts of the Great Recession." *Business Review*, Q2 2013. https://www.philadelphiafed.org/-/media/research-and-data/publications/business-review/2013/q2/brq213_the-diverse-impacts-of-the-great-recession.pdf.

Nelson, Cary, ed. "The Great Depression." University of Illinois at Urbana-Champaign, 2009. http://www.english.illinois.edu/maps/depression/depression.htm.

Ng, Alfred. "Worldwide Ransomware Hack Hits Hospitals, Phone Companies." *CNET*, May 14, 2017. https://www.cnet.com/news/england-hospitals-hit-by-ransomware-attack-in-widespread-hack.

Post, Charlie. "Their Crisis, Our Consequences." International Viewpoint, October 2008. http://www.internationalviewpoint.org/spip.php?article1540.

Prins, Nomi. "Here Comes the Next Financial Crisis." *Nation*, February 1, 2018. https://www.thenation.com/article/here-comes-the-next-financial-crisis.

Pritchard, Carolyn. "Cracks in the System." *New World*, 2009. http://journalism.berkeley.edu/ngno/reports/newworld/cyberterrorism.html.

Salami, Iwa. "Why Unregulated Cryptocurrencies Could Trigger Another Financial Crisis." *Conversation*, January 10, 2018. https://theconversation.com/why-unregulated-cryptocurrencies-could-trigger-another-financial-crisis-89808.

Sands, David R. "Financial Crisis Reshapes World Order." InfoWars. com, October 12, 2008. http://www.infowars.com/financial-crisis-reshapes-world-order.

Shapiro, Robert. "Al-Qaida and the GDP: How Much Would Terrorism Damage the U.S. Economy? Less Than You'd Expect." *Slate*, February 28, 2003. http://www.slate.com/id/2079298.

Silverstein, Sara, and Trevor N. Cadigan. "Ken Rogoff on the Next Financial Crisis and the Future of Bitcoin." *Business Insider*, January 31, 2018. http://www.businessinsider.com/rogoff-next-financial-crisis-cryptocurrencies-bitcoin-2018-1.

Stopsky, Fred. "Doomsday Scenario-China-U.S. War." *The Impudent Observer*, January 22, 2008. Retrieved February 25, 2009 (http://theimpudentobserver.com/world-news/doomsday-scenario-china-us-war).

Tabuchi, Hiroko. "Walmart's Imports from China Displaced 400,000 Jobs, a Study Says." *New York Times*, December 9, 2015. https://www.nytimes.com/2015/12/09/business/economy/walmart-china-imports-job-losses.html.

Tiller, Martin. "What Is a Cryptocurrency?" *Nasdaq*, January 25, 2018. https://www.nasdaq.com/article/what-is-a-cryptocurrency-cm910816.

Watson, Patrick W. "The Threat of a Trade War with China That Nobody Is Talking About." *Forbes*, April 16, 2018. https://www.forbes.com/sites/patrickwwatson/2018/04/16/the-threat-of-a-trade-war-with-china-that-nobody-is-talking-about/#1c1f85e6352b.

Weimann, Gabriel. "Cyberterrorism: How Real Is the Threat?" U.S. Institute of Peace, December 2004. http://www.usip.org/pubs/specialreports/sr119.html.

Werner, Erica, and Renae Merle. "Senate Advances Plan to Weaken Dodd-Frank Banking Rules on Bipartisan Vote." *Washington Post*, March 6, 2018. https://www.washingtonpost.com/business/economy/senate-advances-plan-to-weaken-dodd-frank-banking-rules/2018/03/06/286dbce8-215a-11e8-badd-7c9f29a55815_story.html?utm_term=.5444b8356574.

"World Economic Outlook (April 2018): GDP, Current Prices." International Monetary Fund, IMF DataMapper, April 2018. http://www.imf.org/external/datamapper/NGDPD@WEO/OEMDC/ADVEC/WEOWORLD.

Zetter, Kim. "An Unprecedented Look at Stuxnet, the World's First Digital Weapon." *WIRED*, November 3, 2014. https://www.wired.com/2014/11/countdown-to-zero-day-stuxnet.

INDEX

Page numbers in **boldface** are illustrations.

ABOUT THE AUTHOR

Erin L. McCoy is a literature, language, and cultural studies educator and an award-winning photojournalist and poet. She holds a master of arts degree in Hispanic studies and a master of fine arts in creative writing from the University of Washington. She has edited nearly twenty nonfiction books for young adults, including *The Mexican-American War* and *The Israel-Palestine Border Conflict* from the Redrawing the Map series with Cavendish Square Publishing. She is from Louisville, Kentucky.